Then & Now
Leatherhead & District

Then & Now
Leatherhead & District

Linda Heath and Peter Tarplee

TEMPUS

Frontispiece: The view towards Leatherhead from Hawks Hill, *c.* 1850.

First published 2005

Tempus Publishing Limited
The Mill, Brimscombe Port,
Stroud, Gloucestershire, GL5 2QG
www.tempus-publishing.com

© Linda Heath and Peter Tarplee, 2005

British Library Cataloguing in Publication Data.
A catalogue record for this book is available from the British Library.

ISBN 0 7524 3680 5

Series design and typesetting by Liz Rudderham.
Origination by Tempus Publishing Limited.
Printed in Great Britain.

Contents

An aerial view of Leatherhead town centre, 1935.

Acknowledgements

Many people have generously supplied us with photographs and information and without their help this book could not have been produced.

We can do no more than to list the names of individuals, groups, societies, etc. below, but we hope that all those who have helped us in so many ways will realise that they have contributed not only towards the compilation of this book, but also to the recording of local history.

Individuals include:
  Julia Browne, Bill Culley, Steve Dennis, Gwen Hoad, Sarah Kent, Alan Pooley, Goff Powell, Alun Roberts, Margaret Sowerbutts, Ed Tims, Peter Wells, Alison Wright.

Groups include:
  All Saints School, Ashtead Choral Society, Fetcham Village Infant School, Leatherhead Football Club, Leatherhead Golf Club, Leatherhead Choral Society, Leatherhead Operatic Society, Mole Valley Silver Band, St Mary's School Leatherhead, Surrey Fire and Rescue Service, Therfield School Drama Department.

Photographs on pages 19, 22, 31 and 86 are reproduced by kind permission of Surrey History Service.

Introduction

Many of the photographs in this book are taken from the collection of the Leatherhead and District Local History Society but we have received much help and information, as well as loans of photographs, from many people. Our society owns many hundreds of old photographs of Leatherhead and the surrounding villages, but comparatively few contemporary views. It is amusing to realise that if another 'Then & Now' book is produced in 50 or 100 years' time, all our 'Now' illustrations will be the 'Then' photographs!

The Leatherhead and District Local History Society has, over its sixty years of existence, endeavoured to put as much local history information as possible into the public domain by its publications and those of its members. The present volume is intended to illustrate the changes that have taken place over the past century or so in Leatherhead and its adjoining villages. We hope that we will provide reminders to many of what used to be, and explanations to others of what existed before some of the recent buildings and constructions.

Many large houses have disappeared or been put to new uses. We have tried to demonstrate some of these and, perhaps, explain the naming of some roads or buildings where the original property is no longer standing. Changes inevitably occur with schools and we hope that the juxtaposition of the old and new will reflect some of the changes which have taken place over the lifetime of many of us. Churches are perceived as more constant than many buildings but even here it may be surprising to notice the changes which have occurred since photography started.

The shopping streets of Leatherhead and its environs have changed considerably; in some places the shopping facilities have increased but in smaller areas the number of shops has decreased. Newcomers to suburban Surrey do not always realise that years ago when the places were less populated there was, in fact, more industrial activity. We have tried, where suitable images were available, to record some of these, as we feel that they form an important part of the history of the area.

The fire service in Leatherhead was initially manned by volunteers using a horse-drawn fire appliance which was originally kept in the tower of the parish church, but in 1860 a fire engine house, later known as the clock tower, was built in North Street. By 1926 the brigade had a motorised engine and a new fire station was built to house it. This served the town until 1969 when a new station was built in Cobham Road, Fetcham, suitable for housing modern appliances and the necessary full-time crew.

The railways came to Ashtead and Leatherhead in 1859 after much pomp and ceremony and now the site of the original station is commemorated by Buffers Lane. It was eight years before the line was extended to Dorking and another eighteen before trains were seen at Bookham and Effingham, as the present Bookham station was originally called.

Buses came to the area early in the last century, with the local bus garage being built in 1924. This, like most old London Transport depots in the area, has now been demolished.

So the progress of transport from horse-drawn vehicles is noted as well as the rise and fall of bus travel and the changes in railway trains and services.

Other public services appeared: water in 1884, gas in 1851 and electricity in 1902. The first waterworks, the gasworks and the power station are now all gone and we have tried to place on record some of the history of public utilities locally.

Manufacturing and other industries have all but gone from suburban Surrey but we feel that it is of interest to pay due regard to what industrial processes took place in and around Leatherhead before nearly all the employment was in offices or shops.

Even while this book was in preparation changes were occurring, for example the 'Now' photographs for Bookham locations had to be changed, once when the old goods shed at the station was demolished and again when the New Atlas Works was totally destroyed by fire. Also Norbury Park needed a new 'Now' picture following the recent fire there.

Inevitably, readers will wonder why certain pictures were not included in this book. It has been impossible to include all the ones which we wanted to because of sheer lack of space, but we hope that the ones we have selected will be of interest to all our readers and will provide a little glimpse into the past of this area.

Linda Heath and Peter Tarplee
July 2005

1

Places of Special Interest

*T*here are so many 'places of special interest' that it is impossible to include all of them. We hope that some of your favourites are included here and that all of them will be of interest.

Leatherhead Bridge, with its fourteen arches, has always been a popular subject for artists and this photograph is of a watercolour painted by John Varley in 1832. This view is from the Fetcham side of the river, in front of where Wallis Mews flats are now. Although a somewhat romanticised view, the church can still be seen from there in winter when the trees are bare. The bridge stands on ancient piers, but was largely rebuilt in 1783 by the county surveyor, George Gwilt. It was he who provided the little refuge places for pedestrians. People with horses and carts mainly crossed the river by the adjacent ford, which had the benefit of providing a drink for the horses and a means of washing the carts. The bridge is still one of the finest features of the town.

*T*oday's scene presents a very different picture from the photograph of Bradmere Pond in the Kingston Road in Leatherhead just over 100 years ago. Bradmere Pond is shown on all early maps of Leatherhead and was much used as a drinking place by horses and cattle. In the early photograph Bradmere Cottage can just be seen, almost encased in ivy, and part of it appears on the far left in the modern view. For many years there was a laundry here run by a Mrs Jelley, and some washing can be seen drying on lines behind the pond.

When the pond was filled in, around 1905, a private benefactor provided a drinking trough nearby. In 1964 it was bought privately, but it has recently been given to the council and placed on the pavement in front of the parish church.

The pond site was occupied for many years by Thorne's Garage, later a Heron Garage and now Shell. The block of flats on the corner of Park Rise was built in 2002.

*I*n 1901 land was bought in Leatherhead for a School for the Blind which had been founded in Southwark in 1799. By 1904 the new building was completed with accommodation for 250 residents. It was given a royal charter and then became the Royal School for the Blind. Although reputed to be the finest in Europe it was extremely institutional, with the sexes strictly segregated during both day and night. Reminiscences by former residents of the severe conditions and discipline are heartbreaking to read.

By the 1970s long dormitories were being replaced by single and double rooms; then flats were built for residents and the first wedding took place in 1982. It was also being realised that isolation from the community was not necessarily the best answer, so many of the former residents now live in the town. The school was renamed 'SeeAbility' but the building itself, seen in the current photograph, has now been converted into flats, called Lavender Court.

*I*n the seventeenth century Ashtead Pond was known as the Oxmoor Pond because oxen grazed the adjoining land. By the nineteenth century there were several ponds on both sides of Barnett Wood Lane which were described as old gravel pits. It is possible that they had been dug out to obtain gravel for building the railway. At that time there were no buildings along Barnett Wood Lane, which entered the Wood Field at the south-west corner and continued across it to Woodfield Lane.

Up to the end of the nineteenth century, the pond was twice the size it is now and children used to skate on it in the winter. In the earlier photograph, taken around 1900, Woodfield Farm can be seen across the pond in the left hand corner. It was demolished in the 1930s and a car service station stands on the site now.

Ashtead Park was the medieval manor house of Ashtead and was visited several times by Samuel Pepys. It was bought in 1680 by Sir Robert Howard, who was described as 'not ill-natured but insufferably boring'. By 1684 he had built the present house to the south-east of the old one, planted avenues of trees, made fountains and gardens, enclosed the parkland and installed a herd of deer. So he achieved a good deal in spite of being boring!

In 1790 the house was partially rebuilt and the wings were added around 1880 by Sir Thomas Lucas, providing a billiard room and banqueting hall as well as a tropical conservatory. The Greek banker, Pantia Ralli, acquired the manor in 1889 and he proceeded to modernise the house with electricity and created the lake in the grounds. He had eight cars and he and his wife entertained on a lavish scale. After Ralli's death in 1924 his widow sold the property and the City of London Freemen's School moved there in 1926.

*R*eturning to Leatherhead, The Mansion in Church Street was built in 1739 but stands on the site of a much earlier house. In the sixteenth century it was owned by Edmund Tylney, Master of the Revels to Queen Elizabeth I, who dined there with him on 3 August 1591. The present building was occupied in the early nineteenth century by another courtier, William Wade, this time Master of Ceremonies at Bath and Brighton to the Prince Regent. From 1846 until around 1876 it was a boys' boarding school called the Leatherhead Grammar School. This school had a very high academic reputation and was founded and run by Joseph Payne, an extremely liberal and progressive headmaster.

In 1950 the building became the public library until 2000 when it became a register office. Both these views show the back of The Mansion, which has gardens sloping down to the River Mole, making it a very popular venue for marriages.

*J*ust along from The Mansion is Hampton Cottage, home of the Leatherhead Museum. It is a seventeenth-century timber-framed building and, at the time of the earlier photograph, Hampton Cottage and Devonshire Cottage next door were occupied by Albion and Caroline Ockenden and their family. Duke and Ockenden ran a well-boring business and their sign can be seen above the door. From 1846 the cottage had been used for Strict Baptist services, continuing until the 1860s. When the new Baptist chapel was built in Church Road in 1869 the first pastor was James Ockenden, a cousin of Albion.

From 1918 onwards the cottage was occupied by the Barnard family. Hilda Barnard, who carried on a dressmaking business there, was the last occupant in 1975. The following year it was acquired by the Leatherhead Museum and Heritage Centre Trust and converted, almost entirely by volunteers, into a museum which opened in 1980. This year, 2005, is its silver jubilee and various events are taking place to celebrate the occasion.

*T*his large house, Sunmead House, was demolished around 1935. It was situated on the north side of Guildford Road, Fetcham just to the rear of where Sunmead Parade is now. It has been described as a Regency house with a later addition of a Georgian front. Maps confirm that it was built between 1791 and 1813 in the 'Sun Mead', which originally belonged to the Rising Sun next door. Its occupants were generally of comfortable means; for example, Henry Buxton Sheldrake, a retired land agent, who was there from 1872 until 1906, owned much land outside the parish while his wife, Harriet, was the owner of Stoke Cottages in Cobham Road.

The house was replaced by the present parade of shops between Pang's Villa (the old Rising Sun) and Juniper House.

*E*lmer House was a picturesque Georgian residence which was screened from the road by high brick walls and stood in 36 acres of gardens and parkland on Hawks Hill. It was lived in by W.J. Thompson until 1910 when he retired. He then sold it to Miss Amy Lyle who died in 1921. The house was later lived in by H. Leader Sturt before its demolition in the 1920s. When the house was sold in 1910, 10 acres of land on the north of Guildford Road were disposed of separately as a large building plot.

In 1927 the local water company needed to build a water-softening plant following their amalgamation with the East Surrey Water Company. As they had no available land on the site of the waterworks they used part of the grounds for their new installation. Hence the softening plant is known as Elmer Works and the houses at the east of the site are Elmer Cottages, forming part of what is now Elmer Close.

Mark Oak Gate – shown on some maps as Marked Oak Gate – is on the Cobham Road between Fetcham and Stoke D'Abernon. The gate was on the parish boundary between Fetcham and Bookham and these views were taken from the Fetcham side.

The house, Mark Oak Cottage, is seen to be in Bookham parish.

Beyond the house is the National Trust property of Bookham Common, and the track from the house is Mark Oak Lane which leads to The Glade and Commonside. Behind Mark Oak Cottage there used to be the Peacedene Tea Gardens running from one of the other houses in the row along Cobham Road.

W oodlands Park, just over the parish boundary into Stoke D'Abernon, was extensively altered in 1885 by Frederick Bryant, and the earlier photograph was taken during the building works. Frederick Carkeet Bryant was one of four sons of William Bryant who, with Francis May, was the import agent for the Swedish match manufacturers Carl and Johan Lundstrom, from whom they subsequently bought the patent for making safety matches.

In 1900 Woodlands Park belonged to F.C. Benson, a Bond Street jeweller, but before the First World War it was acquired by E.L. Ralli. He lived there until 1929, when the estate was broken up and the house became a hotel. In 1939 it was an old people's home, in 1975 a residential educational centre, and now it is again a hotel. The fine collection of brick-built farm buildings on the other side of the road survives.

*E*astwick Park, in Great Bookham, was built in the late eighteenth century. Originally it stood in 380 acres, extending from St Nicolas' churchyard to beyond Eastwick Drive. In 1831 it was bought by David Barclay of Barclay Perkins Brewery and then by William Keswick in 1882. He became MP for Epsom in 1891 and lived at Eastwick Park until his death in 1912. The original drawing dates to this period. In the mid-1920s Eastwick Park was bought for a boys' preparatory school from Worthing called Southey Hall, which remained there until German bombing raids forced it to be evacuated in 1941. The lodge, to the right of the main gate, was demolished by one of the bombs. In 1946 the school returned, but closed in 1954 and the house was pulled down soon afterwards.

Eastwick Junior and Infant Schools now stand on the site of Eastwick Park, and Southey Hall School is commemorated by Southey Court sheltered housing, just beyond the trees in the modern picture.

*T*his mansion, Bookham Grove, is near the corner of Dorking Road and Lower Shott. Originally the site of four cottages, the house was built by Vice Admiral Thomas Broderick in 1765. He had retired after a distinguished naval career that began in 1723. Broderick died in 1769 and after changing hands a couple of times the house was bought by John Dawnay, Viscount Downe, and remained in the Dawnay family until 1897.

The grounds of Bookham Grove extended to over 40 acres and stretched to Guildford Road, which had been diverted from its original course where Lower Shott is now. The last private owner was Mrs Silverberg, who changed her German-sounding surname to Hayward during the First World War. She remained at Bookham Grove until 1947 when the house and grounds were bought by Leatherhead Urban District Council to build the Grove estate.

Some years later the house was converted into eight luxury apartments with a range of one and two bedroom homes built close to it in the remaining grounds.

This view of Norbury Park was taken during its occupation by Thomas Grissell, a railway contractor who obviously used his specialist knowledge to good effect when he gave permission for the line from Leatherhead to Dorking to pass through his land. He laid down so many conditions that he achieved an attractive tunnel, a level crossing, as well as a local station of high architectural merit.

Among later owners of the house was Leopold Salamons who donated a large part of Box Hill to the nation. He died in 1914, apparently intending also to donate Norbury Park. When the whole estate was put on

the market in 1930 Chuter Ede, at that time chairman of the county council, immediately arranged for it to be bought by Surrey County Council who have retained the park for the public ever since. The mansion was bought by Marie Stopes and is still in private hands.

During the preparation of this book in March 2005 the house was severely damaged by fire affecting the roof and upper floors.

2

Transport and Services

The growth and development of many of our public services is depicted in the photographs in this chapter. The fire service has changed from volunteers using a horse-drawn fire appliance through to the modern engines in use today, together with the full-time professional crew.

The railway came to the area in 1859 with the line constructed by the Epsom and Leatherhead Railway. Rail transport to the area remains good, but services to passengers have declined as stations have less staff. Bus services came early in the twentieth century and declined at the end of the century as more of the public had their own transport.

Before trains or buses the only means of travelling long distances was by stagecoach and this view of *The Venture* travelling through Ashtead driven by Alfred G. Vanderbilt gives an impression of The Street in the days before it was packed with motorised vehicles.

The first public water supply arrived in 1884 when a pump-house was built between Waterways Road and Bridge Street in Leatherhead. A second pumping station was built in 1935 and this reinforced concrete building survives at the western entrance to the town. Close to the waterworks the Leatherhead and District Electricity Company opened its power station downstream of Leatherhead town bridge in 1902.

*T*he Leatherhead and District Waterworks Company opened its first works in 1884 between Waterways Road and Bridge Street, where they had sunk a borehole and built a pump-house. The pumping station initially contained two 30hp steam-driven pumps which lifted the water the 210ft to a reservoir which had been constructed at the top of Reigate Road. This was the service reservoir supplying water to the parishes of Leatherhead, Mickleham, Ashtead, the Bookhams, Fetcham, Stoke D'Abernon and Cobham. The Reigate Road reservoir was abandoned after a larger one opposite Highlands Farm had been built in 1897, and enlarged in 1909, to replace it. This reservoir is still in use.

The Leatherhead Company was absorbed into the East Surrey Water Company in

1927 and eight years later they built a new pumping station adjacent to the original one. This new station, built in reinforced concrete, was extended in 1940 and it survives to 2005. The earlier works were demolished in 1992 and replaced by the housing development in Wallis Mews, seen here from Waterways Road.

*L*eatherhead's first power station was built in 1902 by the Leatherhead and District Electricity Company Ltd. It was situated just downstream of the town bridge by the waterworks and can be seen in this view of Bridge Street. The DC supply was initially only to Leatherhead but it was soon extended to Ashtead, Mickleham and Fetcham; by 1913 they were supplying AC to Cobham, Stoke D'Abernon, the Bookhams and Effingham; in 1925 this was extended to the Horsleys, East Clandon and Chessington followed by Headley in 1927.

In 1925 a new works was built above the bridge, and by 1941 both works had been shut down as the town was fed by bulk supplies from the national grid. The site of the second power station is partly occupied by a showroom and design offices for a company who equip hotels, while the site of the first station has been absorbed into Wallis Mews.

The railways first came to Leatherhead in February 1859, twenty months after a very elaborate ceremony of turning the first sod had been held. This took place after a procession to the site of the station consisting of police constables, navvies on horses, navvies on foot with spades, schoolchildren with their teachers, the band of the militia, scholars and teachers from the grammar school, clergymen and parish officers, the High Sheriff of Surrey, magistrates of the county, the directors and shareholders of the railway company, and visitors. Following a divine blessing, the first sod was turned by Thomas Grissell, company chairman, and the second by John Labouchere, the High Sheriff of Surrey.

The first Leatherhead station was east of Kingston Road and the earlier photograph shows the original engine shed. When it was released by the railway in 1874 it was used as a church, a school (see Chapter 3) and later a car repair depot. It was only recently demolished and homes have now been built on this site, named Buffers Lane.

W hen the line from the first Leatherhead station by Kingston Road was extended to Dorking in 1867, the London, Brighton and South Coast Railway (LB&SCR) built the very attractive station which remains in use today. This Grade II listed station, built of polychromatic bricks with carved stone details and decorative brickwork, survives although the goods shed and signal boxes have disappeared. As with many stations now in service, a lot of the rooms remain locked and the previously available facilities are not usable by passengers. What had been the stationmaster's house is unoccupied and boarded up.

The goods sidings have been removed and they now form the site of the passengers' car park.

*A*t the same time as the station for the Brighton line was built in 1867 the London and South Western Railway (L&SWR) was extended from Kingston Road to terminate at a new station to the west of the L&BSCR station. In 1885 the South Western line was extended to Bookham and Effingham Junction at the same time as the Guildford 'New' line via Cobham was constructed. This necessitated the construction of a second brick railway bridge over the River Mole, although not as decorative as the one built eighteen years earlier. When the Southern Railway was formed in 1923 the two lines ceased to be competitors and so the track layout was altered in 1927 so that the L&BSCR station served all lines and the L&SWR station was closed.

Traces may still be seen of the staircase from Station Road to the L&SWR station. Old Station Approach contains some railway cottages; the site of the station forecourt and buildings is now occupied by Wood and Pickett who specialise in sales, spares, restoration and construction of classic mini cars.

*T*his train on the L&BSCR was photographed in 1885. It is a special train for Charles Henry Gordon-Lennox, 6th Duke of Richmond, to convey his horses and carriages. It is believed to be on the line between Leatherhead and Dorking, near Mickleham, and consists of passenger coaches, horse wagons and flat trucks to carry the road carriages, and illustrates the way in which the gentry would have conveyed their household and belongings once the rail network was established.

The modern image is taken in the same area and shows a Victoria to Dorking electric multiple unit train just after leaving the tunnel in Norbury Park.

When Thomas Grissell, a retired railway construction contractor who lived at Norbury Park, gave permission for the rail extension from Leatherhead to Dorking to pass through his land he laid down a number of conditions.

The line was to be largely in a tunnel whose portals were to be ornamental and a level crossing

was to be provided where the drive to the house crosses the line, and all new buildings were to be painted green. One of these new buildings was the signal box at Swanworth Crossing and pictured here is Mr Rogers, a signalman with seventeen years' experience, in the lane by the pair of gabled cottages built for railway staff on the down side of the line. The crossing has now been reduced to a foot crossing but the original railway houses remain.

Another of Thomas Grissell's conditions to allow the line through his property was that a station be provided at West Humble even though it was so close to Dorking station. The station was very ornate, designed by Charles Driver, with a tall turret rather in the style of a French château. The position of the station was determined by the fact that Grissell did not want it to be seen from Norbury Park, neither did he want it to interfere with West Humble Infant School. One interesting condition laid down by Thomas Grissell was the right for anyone living or staying at Norbury Park boarding the train to insist that it stopped at West Humble.

Initially called 'West Humble for Box Hill' the station name was changed to 'Box Hill and Burford Bridge', then 'Box Hill' and now it is 'Box Hill and Westhumble' in the timetable although the nameboard on the platform reads 'Boxhill'. Although the ornate station buildings remain none is now used by the railway company.

Many of the old images of Leatherhead show the clock tower in North Street which also housed the town's early horse-drawn fire engine. By 1926 a new motorised appliance had been purchased and a purpose-built fire station was constructed at the River Lane end of Belmont Road. The engine was manufactured by Merryweathers and named *Margaret Blades* after the daughter of Sir Rowland Blades. He performed the opening ceremony for the new station shortly before being elected Lord Mayor of London.

The second motorised appliance at Leatherhead was made by Dennis Brothers of Guildford and was named *Margaret Rose* in 1932. The naming ceremony was carried out by Mrs Greville, of Polesden Lacey, who was Princess Margaret's godmother.

In 1969 a new fire station was opened in Cobham Road which was large enough to house the latest appliances and the full-time crew. After the Belmont Road station was demolished it was replaced with private residential buildings known as Holly Court.

*T*his photograph shows the Leatherhead horse-drawn fire engine outside the fire engine house in North Street, *c.* 1905. The town's first fire engine had been kept in the parish church tower and, in fact, the west door had to be widened to allow the engine to get in. The clock tower in North Street was built in 1860 to house the fire engine and the clock was given by the nearby Congregational church to avoid paying the tax on public clocks. Behind the clock tower, which was demolished in 1952, are Sweech House and Lloyds Bank which survive.

One of the fire appliances in 2005 is seen here in the same position in North Street. This is a Volvo FL 614 Major Pumping Appliance powered by a 6-cylinder diesel engine which carries several ladders, 6kW of lighting – some of which is on an adjustable mast – and 400 gallons of water. By this date Surrey County Council had moved away from using the Surrey-manufactured fire engines from Dennis of Guildford.

*E*ven after railways and buses were commonplace some people still retained their private coaches. One such was the American millionaire Alfred G. Vanderbilt who owned the stagecoach *The Venture* which he frequently drove between London and the South Coast, often calling at coaching inns such as the Swan in Leatherhead and the Burford Bridge in Mickleham. Pictured here is Vanderbilt on a trip from St James's Street to Brighton in 1914, driving his stagecoach.

The following year Alfred Vanderbilt was to perish when the *Lusitania* was sunk and, as he had a special affection for the road through Holmwood, his friends erected a granite memorial there which may be seen north of Bushy Croft on the west of the main road with the following inscription:

In memory of Alfred Gwynne Vanderbilt,
a gallant gentleman and fine sportsman who perished in the *Lusitania* May 7th 1915.
This stone erected on his favourite road by a few of his friends and admirers.

It will be seen also to feature a bit from a horse's harness.

W hen buses were first operating in Leatherhead they were stabled in the yard of the Swan Hotel from 1921 and later also at the Bull. The East Surrey Traction Company, as agents for the London General Omnibus Company, were urgently looking for sites for five bus garages in their area and in 1924 they found the site in Guildford Road, Fetcham, just west of the railway bridge. The land was part of a market garden run by Mizen Brothers.

The garage was built to hold twenty-four vehicles under cover, together with the necessary offices and stores, but by 1928 it had been extended to hold a further twelve buses and the roof was also raised. By 1932 the depot was taken over by London General Country Services Ltd to be replaced the following year by London Passenger Transport Board, who also enlarged the building in typical London Transport architectural style.

Eventually this garage was closed by Arriva on 30 April 1999 and following its demolition the site was developed for offices known as United Technologies House and Juniper House.

The early photograph was taken in Ashtead in 1905 and shows George Astridge leading the first horse of these two of his carrier's carts. Astridge's were involved in a number of commercial enterprises in Ashtead including an ironmonger's shop in Woodfield Lane. The carrier's business was based in Woodfield where they operated as general carriers and furniture removers progressing, of course, from horses to motor vehicles.

In the early 1980s they moved from Ashtead to occupy a unit on the Bookham Business Park and flats were built where their depot was in Woodfield. The firm still operates from the Bookham site where they have now been absorbed by D.H. Cox & Son. We show three of their modern vehicles which contrast with those of 100 years ago. Did families have so many fewer possessions in those days?

3

Churches and Schools

*I*n this view of Leatherhead parish church of St Mary and St Nicholas around 1880 the church looks much the same as today, apart from the north transept (behind the tree) which was extended in 1891. The surroundings have changed much more. We are standing between Highlands Road and Poplar Road, with Worple Road on our left and the cottage now known as the White House in front of us. There was nothing on the corner of Worple Road where Hawkins' Undertakers now have their premises, and the flint wall ran alongside the length of the churchyard down to the Dorking Road.

The churchyard also looks very different here, mainly because it was very much smaller then. The big tree marks the boundary. Elm Bank House owned all the empty land in the foreground, and also the little cottage by the flint wall which housed their gardener. The churchyard is now extremely large, with over 2,000 graves, nearly all of which have been recorded and the details placed on the internet.

*T*he early picture shows Beatrice Wellings with her class at the girls' school in Poplar Road, Leatherhead, around 1894. This school opened in 1884 as a Church of England school for girls. It later became Poplar Road First School, and then St Mary's School in 1986 when it moved to its new home in Forty Foot Road. The school building in Poplar Road was then converted into flats.

In 1913 the three Church of England schools, for boys, girls and infants, moved to new buildings in Kingston Road, now Woodville School. History has a way of repeating itself. Although St Mary's School has only existed for twenty years, in 2006 the pupils from St Mary's, All Saints and Woodville Schools will be formed into a new Church of England school. A name for this has not yet been decided, but the new school building is due to open in 2007 in Woodville School grounds, close to where the first amalgamation took place.

When the boys' and girls' schools moved into the new school in 1913 it was known as the Upper Mixed Council School. In 1926 it became the Central School until 1945 and then the Leatherhead County Secondary School. In 1953 a new school opened in Dilston Road which was named Therfield School in 1964. The name was chosen because the site belonged to the medieval manor of Pachesam, presented by King John in 1205 to Brian de Therfield.

As can be seen from these photographs, drama has always played an important part in the life of both schools. The earlier picture is of the cast at the Central School in a production of *Twelfth Night* in 1936. The modern one is of *Sweeney Todd* performed by Therfield School pupils, who recently took part in the Leatherhead Drama Festival where they did extremely well.

*A*ll Saints church in Kingston Road, Leatherhead, was built to cater for the needs of the growing population in the Kingston Road area. It was designed as a 'neat and plain church' by Arthur Blomfield and was consecrated on 23 February 1889 to 'serve as a chapel of ease to the parish church' – in other words, as a daughter church. By 1980, however, the congregation had dwindled considerably, so it was decided to convert the nave of the church into a hall, and to retain the chancel as a church, with sliding doors between them.

Now, as can be seen in the current photograph, another big transformation has just taken place. The chapel has been retained for Sunday worship, though much transformed, and the old pipe organ has been removed. Churches Together in Leatherhead have just converted the hall part of the church into a Youth Project Café, called B Free, for young people in the area to socialise there in the evenings.

*I*n 1877 the vicar of Leatherhead, Canon Utterton, wrote to the Surrey Education Committee saying he was 'desirous of opening a second infant school in an outlying hamlet.' That hamlet was Leatherhead Common, and the school started in a disused engine shed by the railway (see Chapter 2) also used as a church on Sundays. The first headteacher was Emily Upton, pictured here around 1892 with the children. This school became All Saints School when the first building was constructed in 1900, now the North Leatherhead Community Centre. The school moved from there to its present situation in 1978.

In 2006 All Saints School will close as a first school to become a nursery school and the All Saints pupils, together with those from St Mary's and Woodville will be formed into a new school, as described on page 38.

41

*A*lthough the exteriors of churches do not tend to change much, it is a different story with the interiors. The earlier view is of St Giles' parish church in Ashtead from a watercolour painted by Edward Hassell in 1831. The box pews are still there with the font in the aisle and a high wooden pulpit. The chancel is a picture of extreme simplicity compared to the present view. Between 1820 and 1877 the church was transformed, both inside and outside, gradually evolving into its present appearance. There are several family vaults, including that of the Howards (see Chapter 1). While Mary Howard was Lady of the Manor, from 1818-77 she gave generously to both church and village. In 1852 she gave the land and paid for the building of St Giles' School, and she is commemorated by a carving of her head in a corbel over the west door of the church. The cross and fountain at the eastern end of The Street were erected to her memory in 1915.

Ashtead Park, circa 1890.

The City of London Freemen's School

*T*he City of London Freemen's Orphan School was founded in 1854 in Brixton (then in the country!) by Warren Stormes Hale, later Lord Mayor of London. The school was to provide free education and lodging for seventy boys and thirty girls between the ages of seven and fifteen years whose fathers had died but had been freemen of the City of London. The freemen were members of the various guilds in the City.

By the 1920s London had spread out so that Brixton was no longer in the country, and in 1926, nearly eighty years ago, the school moved to Ashtead Park, shown above around 1890 and below after the school moved in. After the move, the word 'Orphan' was removed from the name of the school. During the war years from 1939-45 and the next decade, conditions were still relatively spartan by modern standards, but over the last fifty years extensions in the school buildings and modern technology in the classrooms have made the school unrecognisable from its beginnings in 1854.

*T*he older photograph shows the parish church of St Mary, Fetcham, before the removal of the fine oak screen and stone pulpit in 1977. The stone pulpit replaced an older three-decker wooden one in the second half of the nineteenth century when the old box pews were also removed and a great many alterations took place. The Revd Sir Edward Graham Moon, rector from 1859-1904, instigated many necessary structural repairs – in the early part of the nineteenth century the fabric of the church had been in very poor condition. The south aisle had collapsed in the eighteenth century and the wall had to be blocked in under the arches. The rebuilding of this aisle was one of many repairs carried out during the Revd Moon's time. Others included the roof and the installation of larger windows to provide more light. Most of the stained-glass windows are memorials to members of the Moon family and the east window was dedicated to the rector.

The School. Fetcham

The photograph of the Victorian children at Fetcham Village Infant School is a 'fraud', as it is a modern photograph with the pupils dressed up as Victorians to celebrate the school's 150th anniversary in 2004, but it was too good to resist. So this one is the present-day photograph and that of the building is the old one. The school was built in 1854 as a Church of England school, but run directly by the parish church, not by the National Society, as the church schools in Leatherhead were.

In the photograph of the school, the building on the corner is the oldest part, and is still much the same, except that the bell tower, the wooden fence and the trees have gone. It in fact looks in much better condition today than it did then.

This nineteenth-century Georgian mansion was Great Bookham rectory for many years. In fact, while her godfather, the Revd Samuel Cooke, was the rector, Jane Austen visited this house in 1809 and 1814 as well as at other times. The postcard from which this illustration was taken was sent in 1913, at which time the Revd George Shepheard Bird was the incumbent. He was the son of Arthur Bird who lived at the Grange, Rectory Lane. Subsequently Great Bookham rectory moved to Flushing Farm, then Bocheham House in Church Road. The present rectory is in Fife Way.

The Old Rectory then became a private dwelling and in 1958 a parade of shops was built in front of the building before the house was demolished three years later. A gap had been left in the middle of the parade so that a Cedar of Lebanon tree in the garden of the Old Rectory could be seen. However, this succumbed to the gales of 1987 and in 1999 further shops were built to make the parade continuous.

*T*his building was built in 1928 as the church hall for St Nicolas' parish church, Great Bookham. The Duke and Duchess of York had spent part of their honeymoon at Polesden Lacey in 1923 and the Duchess was to return there to lunch five years later after opening Church House. At this function she received toys from local children to take to the Church of England Children's Society Orthopaedic Home at Pyrford which she was visiting later in the day.

Church House was used for all the normal functions of a church hall such as jumble sales, Guide and Brownie meetings, Sunday school, dances, whist drives and concerts.

During the war the building was used as a first-aid post. In 1947 Leatherhead Urban District Council set up the Bookham Pie Centre in the hall and a post-natal clinic took place there until the 1980s. The hall was demolished in 1978 to be replaced by a block of flats still bearing the name 'Church House'.

*T*his building, in Lower Road, Bookham, was erected in 1911 in memory of Mrs Mary Chrystie who had been a great benefactor to the village as well as an extremely active temperance worker. This building was the village hall for Bookham and had been financed by Mrs Swann of Hawkwood House.

George Cook of Sole Farm House hired the hall in 1925 and later bought it for use for Sunday services and for Boys' Brigade and other church-based activities. Mr Cook

became the first minister of Bookham Baptist church and he converted the hall to a church three years later. A new hall, for Sunday school and other activities, was built to the west of the church with its stone-laying ceremony taking place in 1929.

The church building was completely refurbished in 2001 with a large glass panel being installed at the front.

Memorial Village Hall, Gt. Bookham. A.D. 1912

4

Trades and Industries

*S*urrey is not thought of as an 'industrial' county but there was a surprising amount of industrial activity in times past. From Roman times the London clay to the north of the area has been exploited to make bricks and tiles, and there were brickworks in the area until about 100 years ago. South of Leatherhead there were large chalkpits and limeworks, with our area containing smaller chalkpits and marlpits as well as gravel workings.

A number of products were manufactured in and around Leatherhead ranging from photographic plates to pottery; from steam cars to engines for motorcycles and aeroplanes; from cigarette lighters to vacuum cleaners and from automatic tea-makers to shampoos and pet medicines. This has all but disappeared now and the area is basically a residential suburb with a few offices, albeit a suburb surrounded by open countryside.

People are now able to travel long distances to work and do not have to work close to where they live.

This scene is from one of the workshops in Ronson's factory in Randall's Road, Leatherhead.

The early photograph is from the period 1926-28, when Ashtead Common achieved some prominence because of the activities of a group of archaeologists from the Surrey Archaeological Society led by Captain A.W.G. Lowther. According to press reports, pieces of tiling and earthenware burrowed out by rabbits gave Lowther the clue to evidence of Roman relics in the vicinity. Typically, the *Daily Express* carried the headline 'Rabbit finds Roman Villa' while the *Sutton and Epsom Mail* proclaimed 'Rabbit Burrow Clue to a Valuable Find'.

The whole excavation site has been interpreted as the remains of a Roman villa and bath-house. A Roman tile works was also close by and the villa is assumed to have belonged to the owner of the works and the bath-house to have been for the use of his staff.

The site of the excavation gives no indication now of the Roman site except for the remains of the spoil heap on the left of the picture.

Greville Works was an early Ashtead factory built around 1890 as Mawson and Swann's Photographic Works. After five years it was taken over by Cadett & Neall and within five years they had built two new factories in Ashtead: Crampshaw Works and Victoria Works on the south and north side respectively of West Hill. Greville Works remains as residential property.

This image shows Crampshaw Works on the south side of West Hill. By 1908 the operation had moved to Harrow, and Peto and Radford operated from these works until 1917 when the British Film Stock Company took it over. This company became Brifco Ltd and by the 1930s they were lacquer manufacturers known as Brifex.

Brifex's main product was leathercloth which had a variety of uses from covering bus and coach seats to bookbinding and making passport covers. By 1972 Brifex had closed and the works had been rebuilt as offices for W.S. Atkins, civil engineers. When they left, the building was demolished and the site was developed for housing as Clarendon Mews.

Victoria Works, on the north side of West Hill, was another important Ashtead factory. It was bought in 1912 by W. Galloway & Co. of Gateshead. They used it as a workshop and sales depot for the American-built Stanley steam cars and traded as Stanley Steam Cars Ltd.

Galloway's, who were the sole importers of Stanley steam cars to Britain, had been assembling them at Gateshead for a number of years but they realised that they needed a base in the south of England, hence their moving into the empty works in Ashtead. (Incidentally, before they started making steam cars in America, their business had been the making of photographic plates and violins.)

When the First World War took place the import of the cars became impossible and Stanleys sold off the stock at Ashtead with a 25 per cent reduction: a 10hp model for £295 and a 25hp model for £425. Many steam cars are still working and this shows a 1913 10hp model photographed in use a couple of years ago.

*O*ne of the most interesting activities at Victoria Works was the work of Ashtead Potters Ltd. This was set up by Sir Lawrence and Lady Kathleen Weaver to train disabled ex-servicemen in the manufacture of pottery. They moved to Ashtead in 1923 and soon employed between thirty and forty people. They produced nursery ware decorated with E.H. Shepherd's illustrations for *Winnie the Pooh*. The Wembley Lion modelled by Percy Metcalfe at Ashtead was the official souvenir of the 1924 British Empire Exhibition.

With the Depression, and following the death of the Weavers, the pottery closed in 1935. Following this the works was occupied by Celestion Ltd, makers of loudspeakers, and in 1946 the McMurdo Instrument Company took over the building until 1964.

The site of Victoria Works is now occupied by a home for the elderly, Limetree Court.

*A*nother industrial activity in Ashtead was the Rosary Leather Works, which was south of the railway by the Woodfield. The factory was started at the beginning of the twentieth century by Robert Saunders and Jesse Swabey and our photograph shows a field by the works covered with skins bleaching in the sun; this method was considered at the time to be superior to using chemically bleached leather. This mill was operating before mains gas was available and so they had their own gas-producing plant. The leather works, known locally as 'the skin factory', was renowned for the unpleasant smell it produced.

Ashtead at this time was also well known for providing entertainment and refreshment facilities for day visitors, most of whom came to the village by train. One such establishment was the Rosary which was also south of the railway beside the Woodfield. All trace of the tea rooms and the leather works have disappeared under what is now Woodfield Close.

*F*rom 1926 between one and two tons of artificial silk per day were being made at the works of the Rayon Manufacturing Company in Ermyn Way, an operation which eventually closed due to water shortages and complaints about unpleasant odours from the process.

In 1938 the British Vacuum Cleaner Company moved into the factory to manufacture Goblin cleaners and other appliances. This company had been formed by H. Cecil Booth who had invented and patented the first effective suction cleaner. The company also manufactured large fixed plants which were installed in hospitals, ocean liners, power stations and large buildings such as the Palace of Westminster.

As well as vacuum cleaners Goblin's became well-known for the Teasmade automatic tea-maker. Magneta clocks were also made in this factory.

By 1982 the company, now part of the BSR group, had transferred their operations to Gosport and the Ashtead works were demolished in 1984. In 1990 the new headquarters of Esso Petroleum Company were opened on the site.

*T*homas Gillett, the son of a Bookham farmer, studied engineering and then set up his own engineering works known as the Atlas Works in Little Bookham Street. The business was described variously as 'motor engineer', 'motor, electric and general engineer', 'millwright' and 'engineer'.

In 1912 Tom Gillett turned the business into a limited company, Gillett Stephen & Co. Ltd, in which he held the position of managing director. They carried out much electrical, mechanical and general engineering work and from the outbreak of the First World War the company obtained a large number of government contracts for the production of aero-engine parts.

Gillett Stephen Ltd sold what had become Old Atlas Works in 1947 to the Bookham

Engineering Company who carried out mechanical engineering and steelwork fabrication and welding. They operated in Little Bookham for twenty years before the company moved to Kingston Road in Leatherhead.

The factory was demolished in 1968 and the site is now occupied by flats named The Blackburn.

Merrylands Hotel was a temperance hotel built by Mrs Chrystie in 1885 opposite the newly built Bookham station. She was an ardent temperance campaigner who used to buy up old alehouses in the area and resell them, with restricted use, as private dwellings. During the First World War, Gillett Stephen needed to expand from the Atlas Works in Little Bookham Street. Merrylands Hotel was bought and a factory, the New Atlas Works, was built in the grounds, while the hotel was converted to offices.

Gillett Stephen combined with the Burney and Blackburne company and continued in the New Atlas Works until 1950 when it was taken over by Wildt & Co.

The works were taken over by Photo-Me International in 1989 after the original hotel building had been replaced by a new office block. Here, the servicing of their products was carried out until a fire in December 2004 destroyed the works; the new offices survived the fire, and are still used by Photo-Me but the 1917 factory has had to be demolished.

*I*n 1918 the action for a cigarette lighter was patented in the USA by Louis V. Aronson. By 1927 he was making lighters with the trade name Ronson. Their motto for these single-action lighters was: 'Press it, it's lit – release it, it's out'.

The first Ronson lighters were imported from the USA and serviced in Britain by J. Liddiatt at premises in Grays Inn Road.

In 1939 Liddiatt transferred his business to Dorincourt, pictured here, a house in Oaklawn Road, Leatherhead.

During the Second World War government contracts enabled them to equip their workshops at Dorincourt with a wide variety of machine tools. When the munitions contracts dried up the company was easily able to convert the machines and staff for the manufacture of cigarette lighters under licence.

In 1952 Ronson's moved to a new larger purpose-built factory and Dorincourt was sold to Queen Elizabeth's Foundation. It now houses their Development Centre where they work with severely disabled young people to give them the skills and ability to move on to a more independent lifestyle.

When they left Dorincourt in 1952 Ronson's moved to this larger factory which they had built in Randalls Road. They soon became Leatherhead's largest employer with a staff of between 2,000 and 3,000. Millions of lighters were made in this works, first fuelled by petrol and later by butane. The ignition system originally used flints on a ridged wheel, but electronic methods gradually took over.

A wide range of products as well as lighters was made by the company. Electric toothbrushes, hairdryers and shavers were produced as well as other butane-operated devices such as blowlamps and decorative candles. A display of many of these may be seen in Leatherhead Museum.

The influx of cheap lighters from the Far East, particularly disposable ones, caused the demand for Ronson's high-quality products to drop. The company went into liquidation in 1981 and after the works were demolished a business park was built on the site.

The Swan Brewery in Leatherhead High Street was founded by William Moore in 1859 when he owned the Swan Hotel next door. It remained in the Moore family for a number of years and in 1875 William's son George built the new steam brewery, shown in this picture from the early part of the twentieth century. Older residents can recall the all-pervading smell in the High Street when the hops were brewed.

The brewery had a 60ft frontage on to the High Street with the buildings extending

about 250ft behind. In 1921 the business was acquired by Mellersh and Neale and by the end of the year the operation was closed. The whole site was redeveloped in 1936 when the Swan Hotel was demolished but the office building was used as Barclays Bank, and later as a betting office, until the development of the Swan Centre around 1980 which can be seen in the modern photograph.

*T*his factory was opened in 1947 in Station Road, Leatherhead, on land which Philip Spencer had bought during the Second World War. Neil & Spencer had been operating in Clapham and when their premises were bombed they moved to the White House (now Crosslands) at Effingham. Here they continued with the manufacture of aircraft components and other war equipment, but Mr Spencer had bought this land in Leatherhead

with the intention of continuing to make dry-cleaning machinery once the war was over. He designed a totally enclosed dry-cleaning machine known as the Spencer 'Junior' which had many unique features. Soon this new factory was too small and they opened a second building, Argosy Works, in Kingston Road.

By the late 1980s the demand for their products had declined, so they closed their factories at Kingston and Raynes Park as well as Leatherhead and all their production was moved to Horsham. The Station Road works were demolished and an office for Atkins now stands on the site.

This 1873 view of the forge in Rectory Lane in Ashtead would be typical of the farrier's and wheelwright's shops which existed in many towns and villages at this time.

Wisteria Cottage and Forge Cottage were formed from a medieval hall house built around 1500, making it the oldest house in Ashtead. The cottages were bought by the blacksmith and wheelwright Robert Wyatt in 1880 and sold by his sons John and James, who had succeeded Robert in the business, in 1931.

On the left of the cottage was the forge and farriery while on the other side there was a

thatched wheelwright's shop. There was also a shed containing grindstones, a drilling machine and a lathe. Much of the machinery was driven by a Crossley oil engine. In the yard there was a tyring furnace and platform as well as the tyre-bending machine which can be seen in use. The wheelwright's work diminished as motor vehicles increased in use but Wyatt's continued as blacksmiths until 1950.

5

A Shopping Spree

*P*erhaps nothing changes as frequently as shops do, and we shall see this as we now go on a 'shopping spree' in Leatherhead, Fetcham, Bookham and Ashtead.

We shall start in Leatherhead High Street. Stephen Neate's grocery stood on the western corner of Neate's Alley from 1862-1945. It was a typical old-fashioned family grocer's shop with bacon joints hanging round the walls and sawdust on the floor. Stephen Neate specialised in bacon and pork sausages made from his own pigs, some of which were kept in a small pigsty behind the shop.

After he died the business was carried on by his widow, Mary, and after her death by their daughters. The shop was demolished in 1956, and the site is currently occupied by Blockbuster.

Neate's Alley is named after Stephen Neate, but it was originally known as Dog Alley because of all the dogs waiting for scraps. It has recently been enhanced by an amusing forged-iron archway, depicting the dogs chasing one of Mr Neate's pigs. It was designed and made locally by Lucy Quinnell and her team at Fire and Iron Gallery.

W e are at the old crossroads, looking down Bridge Street towards the river. The earlier photograph was taken around 1918 and the contrast with today's view is considerable. The mock-Tudor building on the right replaced Wild's creamery on the corner of North Street in 1928 and the building next to it is also modern. On the left, the building with the pillars is partly obscured by the lamp-post, but it was Hewlins' chemist and stationery shop in the older picture, now Soulinni's coffee bar. Beyond that was the old Leather House, for many years a feature of Bridge Street. The Ragge and Lloyd families made and sold leather goods there for several hundred years. The house was demolished in 1939 in a Civil Defence exercise, but whether deliberately or accidentally is not known.

Of all shopping products, meat in the old-fashioned butcher's shop is perhaps the furthest removed from present-day supermarket meat items, as we can see in this view of the butcher's shop in North Street, Leatherhead, around 1900. The contrast between the carcasses hung out here in the open and pieces of meat hygienically encased in clingfilm and polystyrene on supermarket shelves could hardly be greater. Imagine the smell and the flies in really hot weather!

The shop in the earlier picture later became Hartshorn with a slaughter yard at the back. There was a small school behind the Congregational church next door, and the parents of some of the pupils complained about the noise and smells from the slaughter yard next door to the school yard where the children played.

In the modern photograph, we can see the mock-Tudor building on the corner of Bridge Street, and the old Congregational church 'beheaded' in 1934 when the building was bought by the Co-operative Society.

Moving on to Fetcham, the earlier photograph dates from around 1910 and shows the post office on the corner of The Ridgeway and Lower Road. Fetcham had a Post Office Receiver before 1845 who collected and took mail to Leatherhead daily, but Mrs Angelina Partridge became the first Post Mistress around 1890. The front parlour served as the post office, along with another room, described later as having 'stuffed ducks and birds in glass cases, dark green bobble-fringed mantle shelf hangings and an all-pervading frowsty damp smell.'

The building was demolished in 1928 as part of the widening of Lower Road and the post office moved to School Lane, then to St Clements before arriving at its present location in Orchard Parade.

St Clements in The Street, Fetcham seen from across Cock Green and the horse pond that was in Cobham Road where Orchard Close now adjoins. Built in 1865 by James Luff and his son John for their growing business, it provided accommodation for the forge and workshop on the left, their respective houses in the centre and another 'shop' to the right.

A sign states 'Alfred Blaker Shoeing General Smith Gas and Water Fitter at Leatherhead'. Alfred took over on John Luff's death in 1865 but eventually the forge closed and, with some alterations, the buildings were converted to the shops that are there today in 2005. However, Pound Cottage, which can also be seen to the right, was demolished in the 1950s.

We have now arrived in Bookham. This 1910 view looking down the High Street gives some indication of the changes which have taken place over the last century in Great Bookham. In this view, the Royal Oak public house is on the left, and it is believed that the gentleman leaning on the gate may be the landlord. Opposite the pub is the smithy run by C.W. Whyatt. Old Forge Cottage was converted into two shops now trading as Cascade, while

the smithy itself was where Brackenbury's ironmongers shop is now. The terrace of houses, Nos 11, 13 and 15, may still be recognised, although they are all now commercial premises.

The steeple of St Nicolas' church is visible above the Crown public house on the corner of Lower Road; in the later view, the steeple may just be seen over the roof of the Old Crown which replaced the earlier hotel in 1932.

HIGH STREET, GREAT BOOKHAM

A look southwards up Bookham High Street in the 1950s shows some similarities with today but there are some significant changes.

The first two shops were built to replace Nos 7 and 9 Walnut Tree Cottages. The first was opened as a greengrocer, now James Ashley, the greeting card shop, while the gentlemen's outfitter Donaldson is now the Red Cross shop. Both the board outside Jesse Davies, the ladies' hairdresser, and on the wall of the old forge building further up the street advertise Brackenbury and Son. They were a builder and a decorator whose later ironmonger's shop still trades at No. 17a.

On the west side of the street, Walker Smith's grocers had traded here from 1909 until the 1970s when it became International Stores, then Gateway and now Somerfield. Further up the road we see the Royal Oak public house which is still serving the folk of Bookham.

*R*eturning to Leatherhead, we are now in Bridge Street, looking up the street at Kingsnorth bakery around 1910, later to become Holmes, then Harrington's. The first two buildings on that side of the road are the same in both photographs, but the last two have disappeared. These included Wild's creamery, the little building on the corner of North Street which, as we saw, was replaced by the mock-Tudor building in 1928. The corner shop of the High Street, formerly Blaker's ironmongery, and the Swan Hotel were both replaced when the hotel was demolished in 1936.

We are now in Church Street looking at what was still a real crossroads in 1980 when the first picture was taken. Traffic could drive along Church Street and continue either into Bridge Street or North Street, though no longer up the recently pedestrianised High Street. The Burton's tailors building had replaced the Swan Hotel in 1939. Taylors' toy shop occupied the ground floor, then Pimms' furniture shop, and now More's stationery and post office. The upper part of the building is now a Travelodge with a model of the swan statue from the portico of the old Swan Hotel. The original statue is in the garden of the Leatherhead Museum in Church Street.

In front of More there is a modern feature of stone, slate and ornamental ironwork recently produced locally by Fire and Iron Gallery. The four iron roundels depict local bridges over road, rail and river. A shopping market, as seen in the current photograph, now takes place here twice a week

*T*here have been many photographs of The Street in Ashtead taken from this vantage point beside the Brewery Inn. The old one, from around 1900, is delightfully uncluttered by either people or traffic and shows all the little shops along the south side of The Street, but only a few on the north side which was still mainly occupied by Street Farm at that time. The ivy-covered house was called The Shrubs and was occupied by George Sayer, landlord of the Brewery Inn.

Apart from the absence of traffic, perhaps the most noticeable difference from the present day is the empty piece of land behind the wooden fence on the corner of Woodfield Lane opposite the Brewery Inn. In the early 1920s this little field was used for grazing the dairy herd belonging to Sidney Wilcox, whose dairy was just across the road. The field belonged to Street Farm, further down the road, but by the late 1920s the present-day buildings had been constructed there.

High Street, Ashtead.

R. Matten.

*L*et us take a look back at the shops on the north side of The Street around 1910. Again, it is the inevitable contrast between one solitary bicycle and the present-day traffic which makes the chief difference between the two photographs. Notice what a small row of shops it was then, with the gates and hedge of Street Farm on the right. In due course, Street Farm was supplanted by an Esso petrol station, which has now, in its turn, been demolished in 2005. On the left hand side, the shops in the modern photograph have been extended forwards, replacing the little front gardens behind the wall. In the distance, on the corner of Rectory Lane where Milner's Carpets are now, were two cottages surrounded by a fence. The one on the corner was pulled down in 1930 to build the Woodcote Motor Garage, which was the first filling and service station in The Street.

We end our shopping trip with a view of Craddocks Lane (as it was then) in Ashtead around 1926. This presents perhaps the greatest contrast of all between then and now, with no shops at all. It is hard to believe that in a relatively short time such a change has been effected. In the earlier view, the buildings are part of the farmyard of Woodfield Farm which stood opposite the pond. The building nearest us was the granary and the one beyond that was a cow shed, with the entrance to the farmyard just behind it. The

sign on the tree on the left was for the Ashtead Football Club which used part of the field as their football pitch. Cows grazed there when there was no football!

The shopping parade on the right in the modern photograph was constructed soon after Woodfield Farm was sold and demolished in 1935, but the one on the left was not built until the early 1950s.

6

Pubs Past and Present

The Cabaret of Elenour Rummyng.

Having been on a pretty exhaustive spending spree at the shops, in this chapter we'll now go on a 'pub crawl' round some of the local hostelries, both past and present. We'll start in Leatherhead at the oldest one, the Running Horse, and progress from the Bull to the High Street, on to Ashtead, then Fetcham, Bookham and Mickleham. Cheers!

The Running Horse by the River Mole is a 'must' on this tour of inns. The building is fifteenth century and is reputed to be the place where the famous ale-wife, Eleanour Rumming, was immortalised by John Skelton in 1528 in his long and very unflattering poem *The Tunning of Eleanour Rumming*. This poem was later set to music by the composer Ralph Vaughan Williams. Eleanour Rumming certainly existed, as there are references to her being fined for selling 'nappy ale' in the sixteenth century.

There used to be a hag-like picture of Eleanour Rumming above the upper window which, alas, has disappeared without trace.

*T*hese May Day celebrations took place outside the old Bull Inn in Leatherhead around 1905. The original Bull public house stood not on the site of the later New Bull Hotel, but across the road at the top of Bull Hill. In 1925 the inn was demolished and the site was then occupied by the Gas Company showrooms, now replaced by an office block called Fairmount House. The Bull forecourt was regarded as something of a 'Speaker's Corner' and many gatherings took place there, including dancing round a maypole on May Day.

It is impossible to take a photograph from the same vantage point today. Fairmount

House is currently undergoing renovations before a new firm moves in. It stands not only on the site of the Bull, but also of the Red House which was behind the inn. This was originally a private house which later became a hotel; it was very popular with Londoners during the 1930s for a week or fortnight's holiday to enjoy the delights of local beauty spots.

Our next call is at the former Swan Inn, or Hotel, a seventeenth-century coaching inn at the foot of the High Street. It was a splendid hotel with extensive grounds, kitchen gardens and orchards. Sadly, it was demolished in 1936 and the present Burton's tailors building erected in 1939. The stone swan from the portico of the hotel is now in the garden of the Leatherhead Museum in Church Street.

The old photograph dates from around 1920. At this time a single room cost 3s per night (15p) and a double room 5s (25p). A fire in the bedroom cost 6d or 1s per day. Cold luncheon was 2s, hot with sweet 2s 6d; dinner 3s 6d.

There is now a Travelodge on the upper floors of the present building with a replica of the original stone swan outside, but there the resemblance to the Swan Hotel ends. The entrance to the Swan Shopping Centre (named after the old Swan Hotel) is on the site of the Swan Brewery offices which closed in 1922.

Our next stop is further up the High Street, on the opposite side, at the King's Head. This stood where Dixons shop is now. In the late eighteenth century it was destroyed by a fire, but rebuilt in 1794. As can be seen in the earlier photograph, it jutted much further forward, making the High Street quite narrow at this point, which is partly why it was pulled down in 1929. The road was then widened and the first Sainsbury store was built there.

The building on the other side of the alley became the King's Head for a time,

then Freeman, Hardy and Willis shoe shop for many years. After various changes, it has now become an Italian restaurant. King's Head Alley has recently been enhanced by an attractive forged-iron archway which can just be seen in the modern photograph. It depicts a king's head, 'churchwarden' pipes and tankards. Like the Neate's Alley archway, it also was designed and made locally by Lucy Quinnell and her team.

High Street, Leatherhead.

We now cross the road again at the Duke's Head, nearly at the top of the High Street. Although the building has a nineteenth-century appearance, it in fact dates from the seventeenth century. In the eighteenth century it was known as the Duke of Cumberland and church vestry meetings were sometimes held here then, though probably not at the bar! In the early twentieth century bands used to perform in front of the pub on Saturday evenings and people would dance there to the music. In the 1930s it was a hotel offering accommodation, a comfortable lounge and teas served on the lawn at the back in summer. There is no lawn at the back now and it is many a long year since it offered bedrooms.

The older photograph is very modern compared to ones published elsewhere showing it in 1850 and in 1905, but as can be seen from the present photograph, although the front of the building has not changed, almost everything else has.

W e now move on to Ashtead where our first stop is at the Brewery Inn which started as a small beer house around 1800. In 1850, at the time of the earlier picture, George Sayer, a member of the Parish Council, was the proprietor of the inn and the brewery

behind it. By 1871 he was employing five labourers, supplying 'genuine ale and porter to the Trade and Families'. After his death in 1888 his son, another George, continued to run it. Many of the alterations to the building were made around that time. In the 1850 view the tall chimney for the actual brewery is very prominent and there were two separate buildings, subsequently joined together. It remained like this until around 1930 when it was rebuilt as it is now.

ASHTEAD BREWERY c 1850 AD

Our second stop in Ashtead is across the road at the Leg of Mutton and Cauliflower pub, known familiarly in the old days as The Leg. There seems to be no record of how it acquired its name – perhaps it was the staple fare offered.

In the earlier view we are looking at the timber-framed structure of the building around 1860 when Thomas Skilton was the landlord. In 1879 he informed his clientele that he had considerably improved its capabilities by providing seven bedrooms and six rooms for public and private use. He described the bedrooms as being 'large and well ventilated; families could have private apartments, and

there was good stabling, providing coach houses and loose boxes for hunters.' At this time the post office was situated here, but by 1882 it had moved elsewhere. The brick frontage dates from the 1890s.

Recently the name of the pub on the sign outside has been abbreviated to LOMAC – a sad sign of the times.

We have now left Ashtead and moved on to Fetcham where we shall pause first at the old Rising Sun, now occupied by the Chinese restaurant, Pang's Villa. This was in the very old building at the corner of Guildford Road and Cobham Road which for many years had a sign on it saying '*c.* 1348'.

The medieval core of the building was much extended, probably around 1800. In 1805 it was described as a 'compact brewhouse, store room and cellar capable of holding 78 butts of beer', i.e. 8,424 gallons! It served as a public house until the 1930s when the new Rising Sun was built on the other corner of Cobham Road and this building then became a café called The Old Rising Sun. During the 1940s it was used for a time as a youth hostel; then it became a restaurant called the Pilgrim's Rest, later Le Pelerin (The Pilgrim) before becoming Pang's Villa.

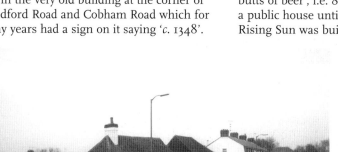

The older photograph shows a group of young people around 1945 when it was a youth hostel.

*T*he old Bell Inn in Fetcham was in what is now the car park of the Bell Inn. It was a popular venue for fashionable weddings and other functions as well as a regular meeting place for the Surrey Union Hunt which kept its hounds in the kennels at Kennel Lane.

The house, like most of the older houses in Fetcham, was originally a farmhouse. It had 8¼ acres of land, 7 acres of which were the fields known as the Matterdons which ran up to what is now Kennel Lane. By 1800, however, the Matterdons had been incorporated into an outlier of Fetcham Park and the house had become the Bell public house. The building was eventually demolished after the present public house was opened in 1937, providing space for a car park.

Both Fetcham's public houses were replaced by new buildings in 1937, both concave-fronted, by Joseph Hill. The other was the Rising Sun, mentioned opposite, which in 2005 is closed and the site awaiting redevelopment.

The Crown Inn was one of the alehouses in Bookham; others were the Fox on Ranmore, the White Hart now Grove Cottages, the Royal Oak in the High Street, the Anchor in Lower Road, the King's Arms opposite the church, Halfway House in Lower Road, and the Castle and Half Moon Cottage in Little Bookham Street.

The picturesque inn with decorated barge boards advertised 'Good Beds, Luncheons and Dinners Provided'.

In 1932 the brewers, Hodgsons of Kingston, demolished the old inn and perversely replaced it with The Old Crown public house. This was a typical 1930s brick-built pub with saloon, private and public bars as well as a jug and bottle department and off-licence.

The off-licence is now a hairdressing saloon and what was the public bar is an independently operated French restaurant, while the remaining bars form the public house accommodation.

The Crown Inn, Gt. Bookham.

"THE WINDSOR CASTLE" LITTLE BOOKHAM.

Moving on to Little Bookham, we pause at Ye Olde Windsor Castle in Little Bookham Street. It is a sixteenth-century building, but the first reference to it as an inn was not until 1806. Henry Weale was the publican from the mid-1860s until his death about twenty years later, when his widow, Mary Ann Weale, was the licensee until 1902. After his death she started a little shop at the far end of the building which then became the business further down the street, which still operates today.

Even into the twentieth century the pub opened at 6.00 a.m. so that agricultural workers could fill their flagons with ale for the day. Livestock were kept outside and many a farm worker must have been greeted by a sleepy cow, pig or sheep on his way to work!

The earlier photograph dates from around 1913 and, as can be seen, both the building and its surroundings have changed considerably.

*O*ur final call is at Mickleham. This photograph was taken in December 1885 and is titled 'Young Saunders and Churchwarden Rose'. It was taken outside the Running Horses public house in Mickleham and we assume that the man with the apron as well as the dog belong to the hostelry.

This is an old seventeenth-century coach and posting inn which was previously known as the Chequers. It is still a very busy and popular public house situated opposite Mickleham parish church on what was the main London Road before the new bypass was built.

7

Recreation and Events

Leatherhead Institute.

The Letherhead Institute (note the older spelling of Leatherhead which gradually fell into disuse) was founded in 1892 by Abraham Dixon, a great benefactor to the town who only came to Leatherhead after his retirement in 1868. He founded the Institute for the education, enjoyment and recreation of the people of Leatherhead and it has been used for these various purposes ever since then. In 1910 it was described as 'The Literary and Scientific Institute, containing reading, billiards and reception rooms, separate rooms for meetings, a large assembly room with a stage, a reference and lending library of 2,400 volumes, and a tennis court in the spacious gardens behind the building.'

Nowadays, a number of rooms are let as offices, but the remaining rooms are still used by many groups for meetings, including the very fine Abraham Dixon Hall and an excellent lending library. It is the home of the Leatherhead Community Association which provides many facilities and excursions for members and arranges the hire of rooms to other groups.

*T*he Leatherhead Operatic Society began in 1904 as a group called 'the Pierrots'. Charles Grantham, a furniture maker in North Street, made superb scenery for their productions, in which he also took part. Performances were often in aid of local causes, such as the newly opened hospital at Victoria House in 1906, later to become a home for the disabled when the present hospital in Leatherhead was built in 1940.

The Pierrots used to perform in the Victoria Hall in the High Street, which later became

a cinema and then a repertory theatre. Their production of *HMS Pinafore* in 1906 was so successful that the group was then renamed the Leatherhead and District Dramatic and Operatic Society in that year with Charles Grantham as chairman, so the society will celebrate its centenary in 2006.

The modern photograph is of their production of *My Fair Lady* at the Thorndike Theatre.

*I*n 1905 Ralph Vaughan
Williams founded
the Leith Hill Festival in
Dorking in which choirs
from villages in the area
competed each year. In
1928 choirs from towns
were also admitted to the
competition for the first time and this was
when the Leatherhead Choral Society came
into being. It took part on that occasion and
has participated every year since. The festival
is a three-day event with a very high standard
of performance and is the highlight of the
year for many amateur singers. Whereas the

Operatic Society (on the opposite page) will
be celebrating its centenary next year, the
Leith Hill Festival is celebrating its centenary
this year.

The Leatherhead Choral Society has won a
number of prizes at the festival. In addition to
taking part in this, the choir holds a variety of
events each year.

The Ashtead Choral Society was founded in 1949 by the baritone George Pizzey who is seen in the earlier picture conducting the choir at their Christmas carol concert in the Dorking Halls in 1959. The pianists were Winifred and Jane Boston. George Pizzey continued to conduct the choir until 1974 when he was succeeded by Arthur Diamond. Over the next twenty years the choir expanded to its present number of 135 singing members and from 1986 onwards a number of continental tours have been undertaken in addition to their concerts in this country. The choir has a smaller group, the Ashtead Singers, who also travel and perform regularly at various venues, including St George's Chapel, Windsor.

The modern photograph shows the choir celebrating its golden jubilee, with pianist Anne Shepherd in the centre and conductors Arthur Diamond and Paul Dodds. The latter became the society's regular conductor in 1998.

*T*he Mole Valley Silver Band can trace its origins at least as far back as 1881. It was known then as the Leatherhead Town Band which performed at many occasions and processions.

It did not play during the First or Second World Wars but it was re-formed in 1947 as the Bookham and District Silver Band, and founder members played for over twenty years.

In 1974 Mole Valley District Council was created and the band then took its present-day title of the Mole Valley Silver Band. It has players of all ages, not only from within Mole Valley, and welcomes new members.

Today the band is still in much demand and plays at many local events, including town festivals, fêtes and charity events. Members have recently enjoyed playing at The Theatre in Leatherhead with the London band, Regent Brass. (Photograph by kind permission of Simon Dorn Photography)

*T*he Leatherhead Golf Club started in 1903 as the Surrey Golf Club, but changed its name in 1908. The original clubhouse stood at the crest of the hill between the Oxshott and Chessington roads, beyond where B&Q is now. Situated on the crest of the hill, it could be seen from almost the length of Kingston Road.

The club thrived and by 1922 there were 484 members. In 1940, however, the clubhouse was hit by a German bomb which destroyed over half of it. At the end of the war things were in a bad condition, both physically and financially, with only about eighty members. In 1952 a new company was formed to run the club and things started to improve immediately.

The big transformation of both the course and clubhouse took place when the M25 was constructed around 1980. This cut right through the course, but with considerable skill and ingenuity, it was completely rearranged. At the same time, the new clubhouse was built, as seen in the modern photograph.

*T*here are references to football matches being played in Leatherhead since the early 1900s. However, the official Leatherhead team, known as The Tanners was not formed until 1946, just two seasons before the earlier photograph was taken. They achieved national acclaim in 1975 when they reached the fourth round of the FA Cup, and again in 1978 by reaching the final of the FA Challenge Trophy at Wembley.

Since 2000 the club has been run by loyal Tanners supporters who stepped into the breach when the team was in financial difficulties. It seemed for a time as if it would have to be disbanded, but the team is now going from strength to strength, supported by a small army of volunteers.

The team ethos is 'A club run by its supporters for the benefit of the community' and the Tanners are very proud that they host Pitstop, a registered charity which provides a daytime drop-in centre for homeless, unemployed and socially isolated members of the community in and around Leatherhead.

*L*ieutenant George Barnard Hankey returning home from the South African War arrived at Leatherhead South Western railway station at about 6.00 p.m. on 5 July 1900 to be met by a large welcoming party.

This picture shows the procession in the southern end of The Street, Fetcham, having just turned down from School Lane; the school hall with its small bell tower may be seen.

Led by Mr Partridge, landlord of the Bell, on the grey horse, and the Bookham Brass Band, the carriage is now being drawn by estate workers while others march in front and alongside accompanying George and his father John Barnard Hankey up to Fetcham Park for the formal welcome. This was a major event in the village.

Although the bell tower is no longer in place, the roof of the school is still visible behind the trees, with Chain Cottage on the left.

*T*here is a nice contrast here between the formality of the post office staff in Leatherhead outside the post office in North Street around 1902 and the present-day staff setting out from the sorting office in Station Road in May 2005.

Before the railway came to Leatherhead in 1859 mail came by rail to Epsom and then by carrier to Leatherhead. The post office was in Bridge Street until around 1900 when the new post office was built in North Street. This has now been converted into a pub named the Penny Black, as a reminder of its former use.

The modern photograph shows the staff about to start their annual sponsored cycle ride from Leatherhead to Littlehampton to raise funds for the Royal Marsden Cancer Campaign. Last year they raised £11,400 and this year they have raised £12,300 at the time of this book going to press. They charge no expenses – every penny goes directly to the fund. Congratulations – well done!

Other local titles published by Tempus

Bookham and Fetcham

LINDA HEATH

This book follows the pictorial history of three villages – Fetcham, Great Bookham and Little Bookham. The images cover every aspect of life in the villages, including stately homes and humble cottages, education, trade, work and recreation. For those who have known Bookham and Fetcham for a long time, this will bring back nostalgic memories, while for newcomers it will provide a fascinating insight into the area's past.

0 7524 1825 4

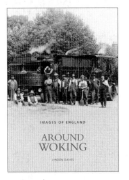

Around Woking

LYNDON DAVIES

This fascinating volume of old images traces some of the developments in Woking during the 1920s and early 1930s. Drawn from the archive of Woking photographer Sidney Francis, this collection of over 200 photographs, many never before published, highlights some of the important events that have occurred in the town during this time, including rare views of Woking Football Club, officials at Brookwood cemetery and visitors to Woking Mosque.

0 7524 3230 3

Walton-on-Thames

WENDY HUGHES

This selection of over 200 archive photographs and postcards illustrates many of the changes that took place in Walton-on-Thames during the last century. In the late nineteenth and early twentieth centuries Walton evolved into a busy town, with inns, schools, hotels, shops and businesses, including Lee's Bakery and William Gray's boot-repairing business. Also remembered are the New Zealand soldiers recuperating in the town during the First World War.

0 7524 3051 3

Roman Surrey

DAVID BIRD

In AD 43, the area of south-east England now known as Surrey became part of the Roman Empire. This book combines both historical and the latest archaeological evidence with topographical studies to build a vivid picture of life at the time, from villas and coinage to beliefs and customs. The changing face of Surrey's landscape is charted, and theories relating to the development and eventual decline of Roman Surrey are discussed.

0 7524 2889 6

If you are interested in purchasing other books published by Tempus, or in case you have difficulty finding any Tempus books in your local bookshop, you can also place orders directly through our website

www.tempus-publishing.com